My Disney Stars and Friends 2

Workbook and eBook

Mary Roulston

Contents

1 At school

1 Match and say. 2 Think and check (✓).

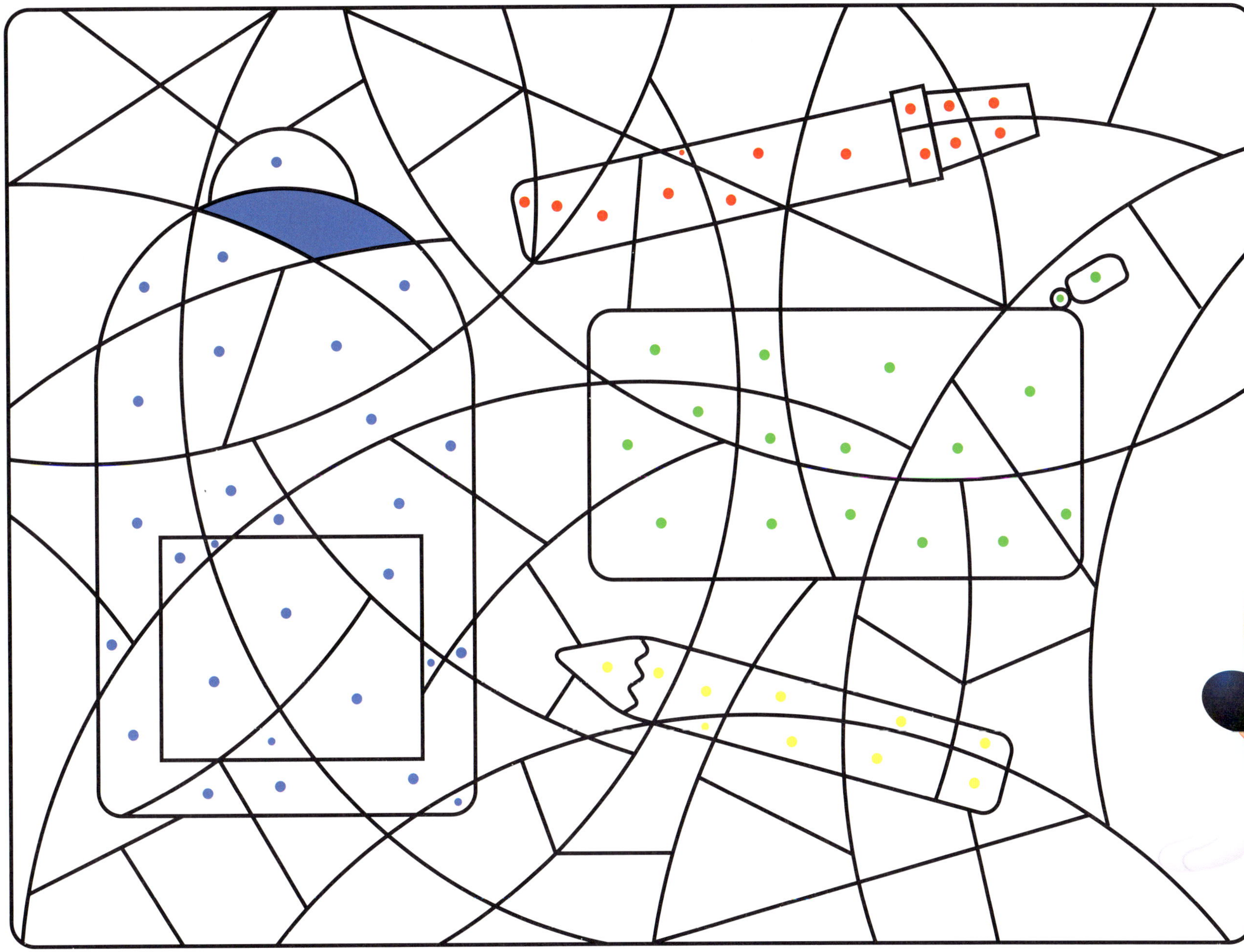

1 **Color and say.**

I'm worried

1 Who is worried? Circle and say. 2 Think and check (✓).

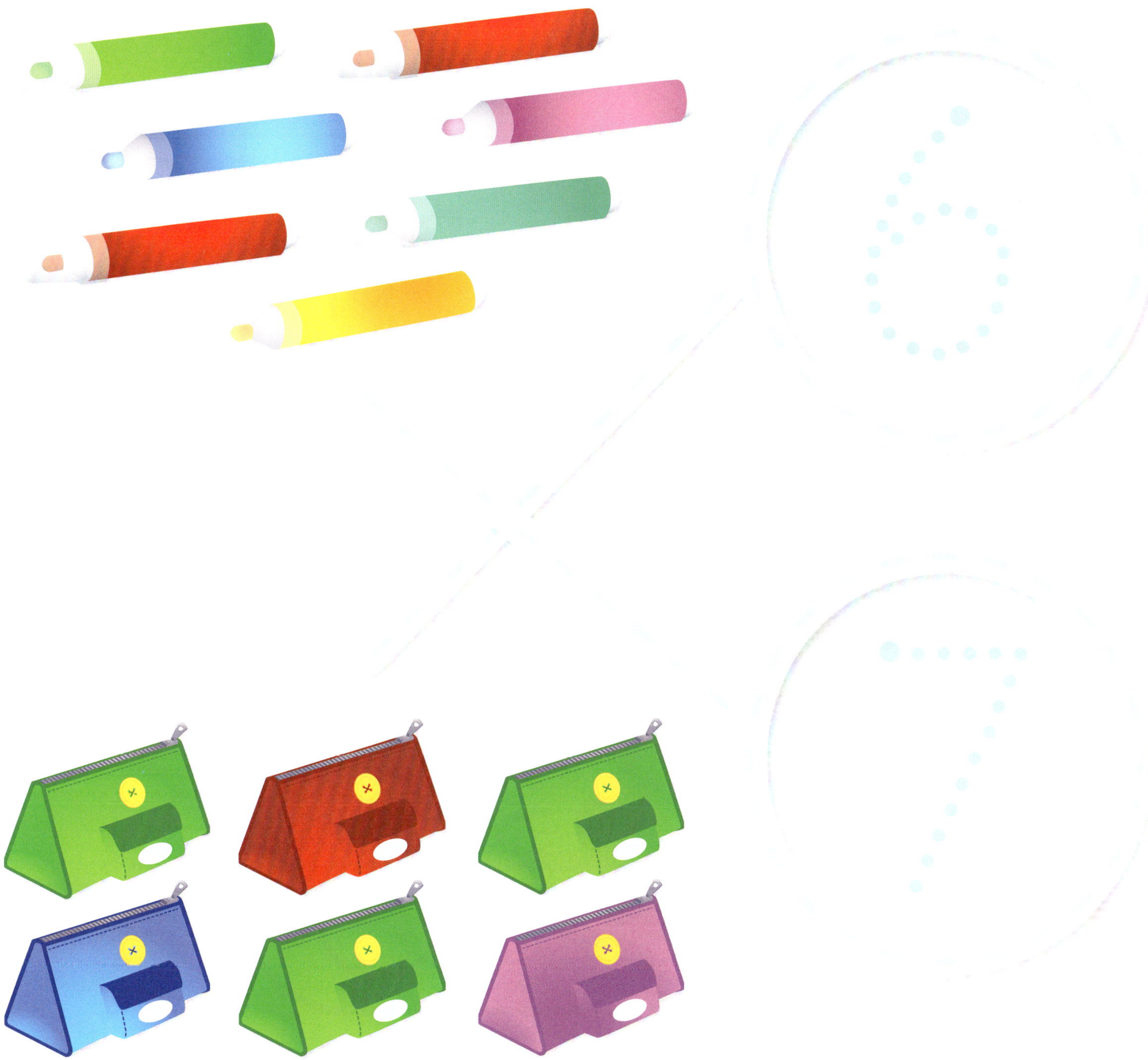

1 Count and match. 2 Trace and say.

Back to school

1 1.10 Listen and check (✓). 2 Look and cross (✗).

1 *I'm kind* **Look and circle.** 2 **Choose and color.**

Schooltime

1 Look and match. 2 Point and say.

1 🎧 1.14 Listen. Find and check (✓). 2 Color your star.

2 The weather

1 Match and say. 2 Think and check (✓).

1 Trace and say.

I'm excited

❶ Who is excited? Circle and say. ❷ Think and check (✓).

① Trace ○ and color ●. ② Say.

Lesson 5A ○ Storytime

Olaf's sunny day

1 2.10 **Listen and check (✓).** 2 **Look and cross (✗).**

1 *I love my friends* **Look and circle.** 2 **Choose and color.**

Weather

❶ **Draw lines.** ❷ **Point and say.**

❶ 2.14 **Listen. Find and check (✓).** ❷ **Color your star.**

3 My face

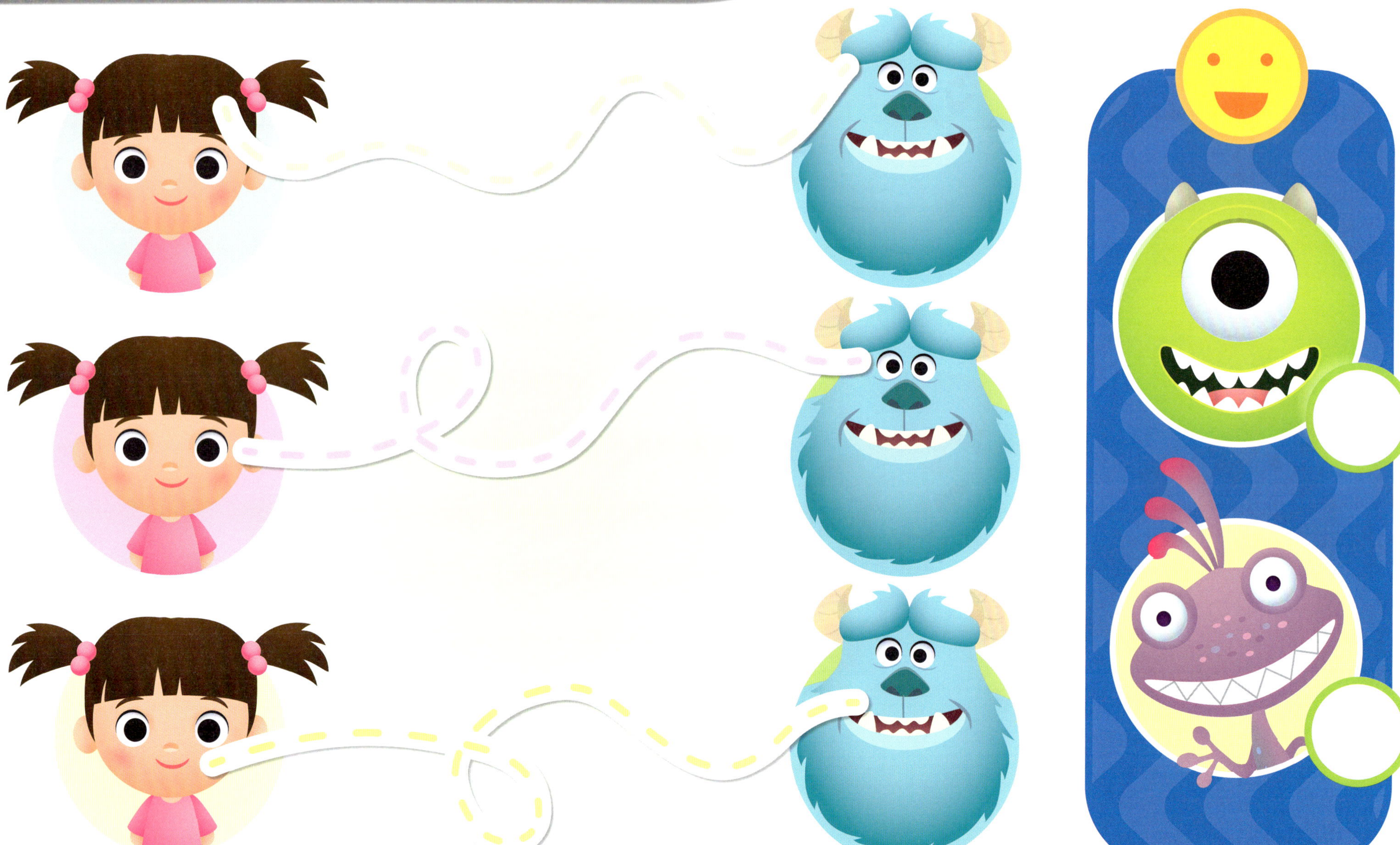

1 Match and say. 2 Think and check (✓).

❶ Trace and say. ❷ Color.

I'm silly

1 Who is silly? Circle and say. **2** Think and check (✓).

1 Trace and say.

Guess who?

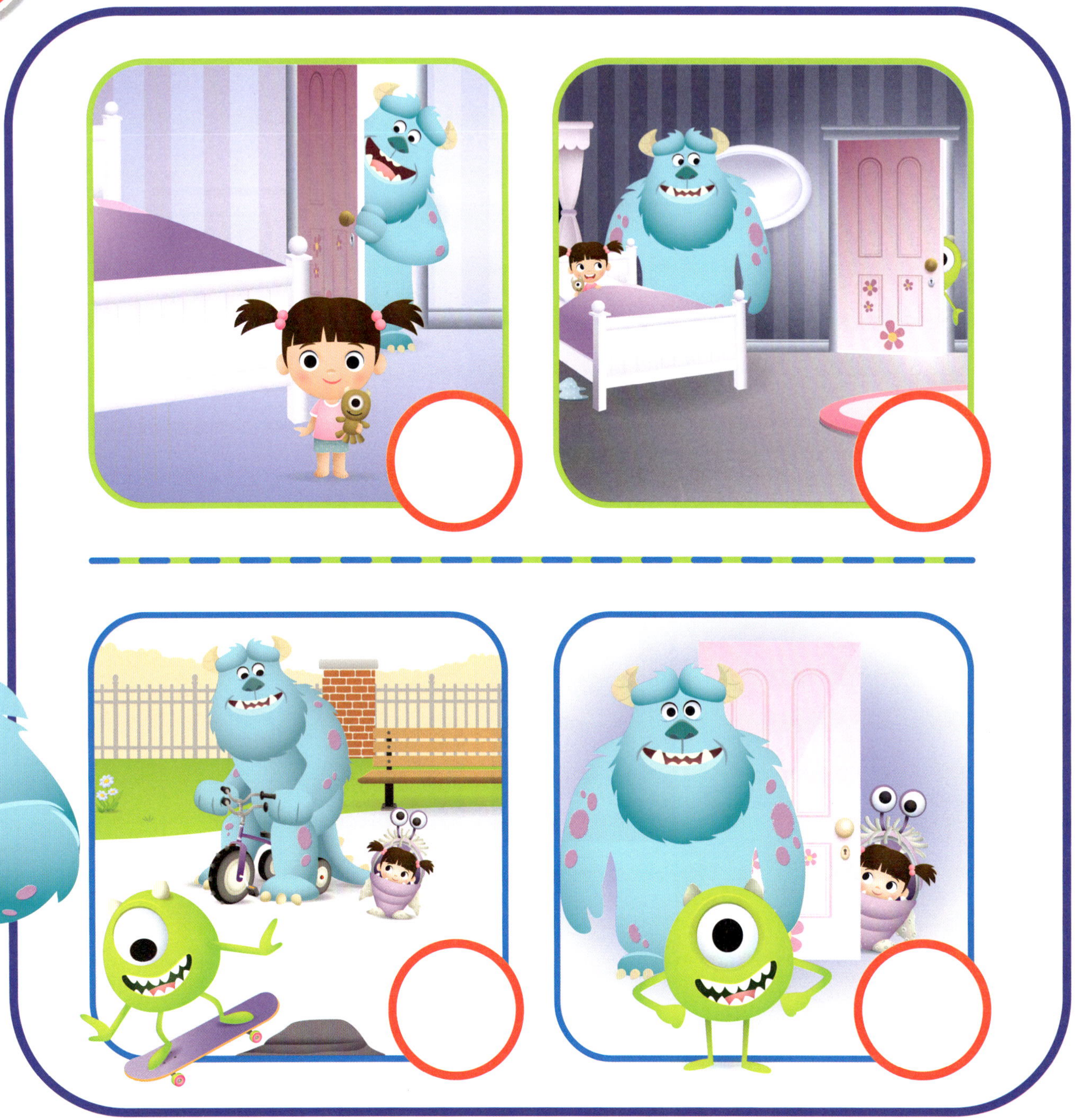

1 3.10 Listen and check (✓). 2 Look and cross (✗).

1 *I love bedtime* **Look and circle.** 2 **Choose and color.**

Faces

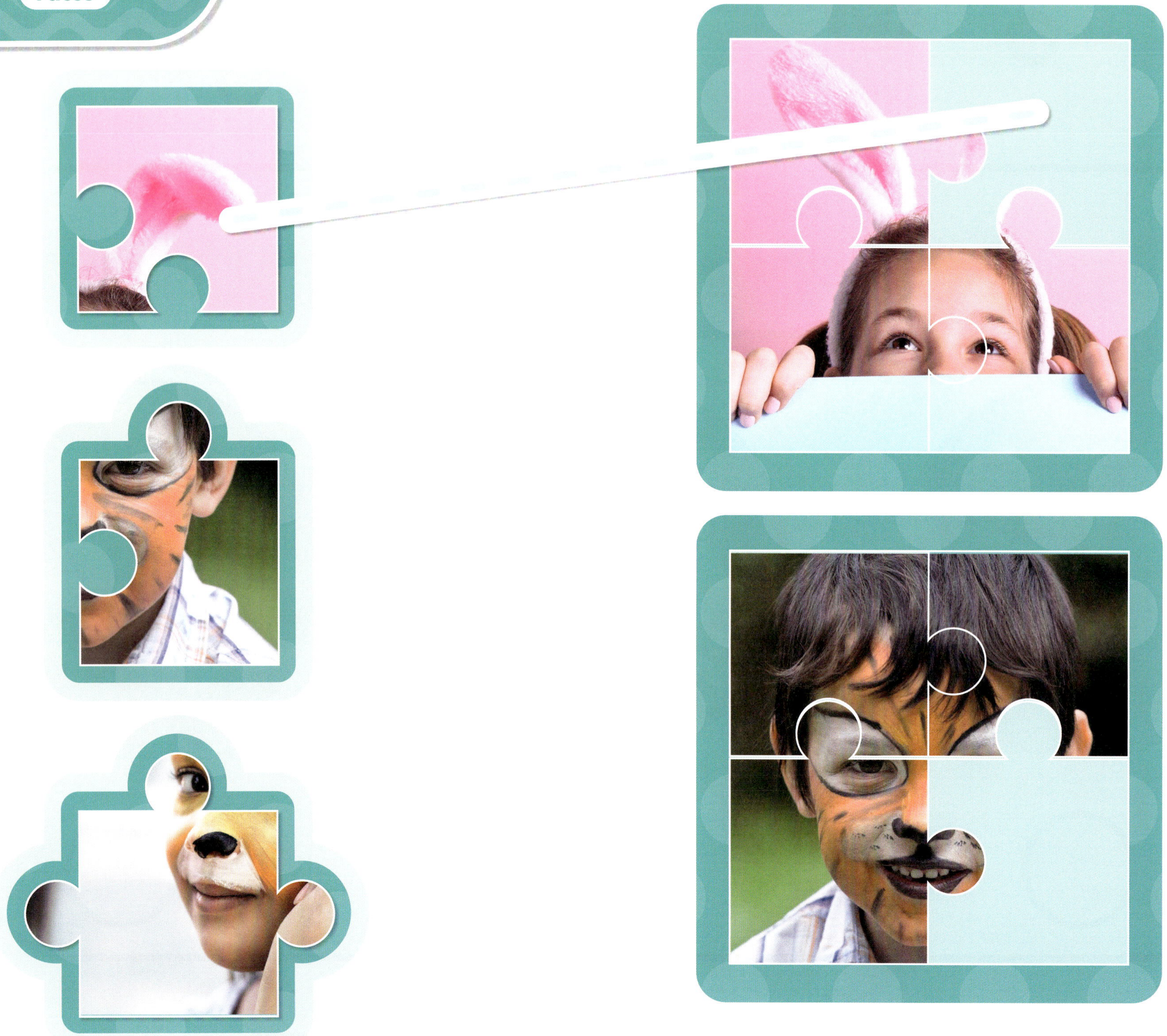

❶ Look and match. ❷ Point and say.

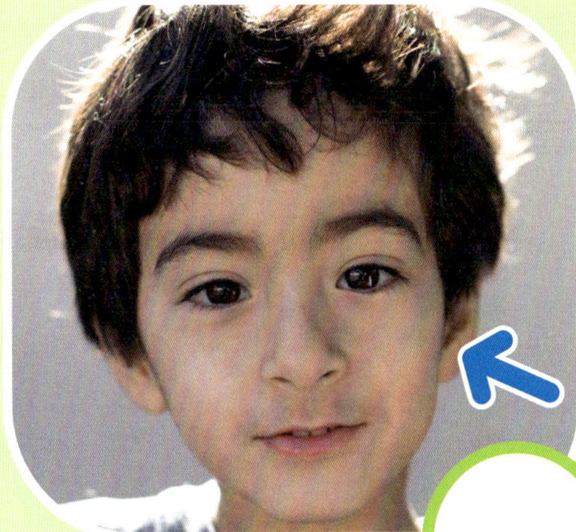

1 3.14 **Listen. Find and check (✓). 2 Color your star.**

4 My things

❶ **Match, say, and color.** ❷ **Think and check (✓).**

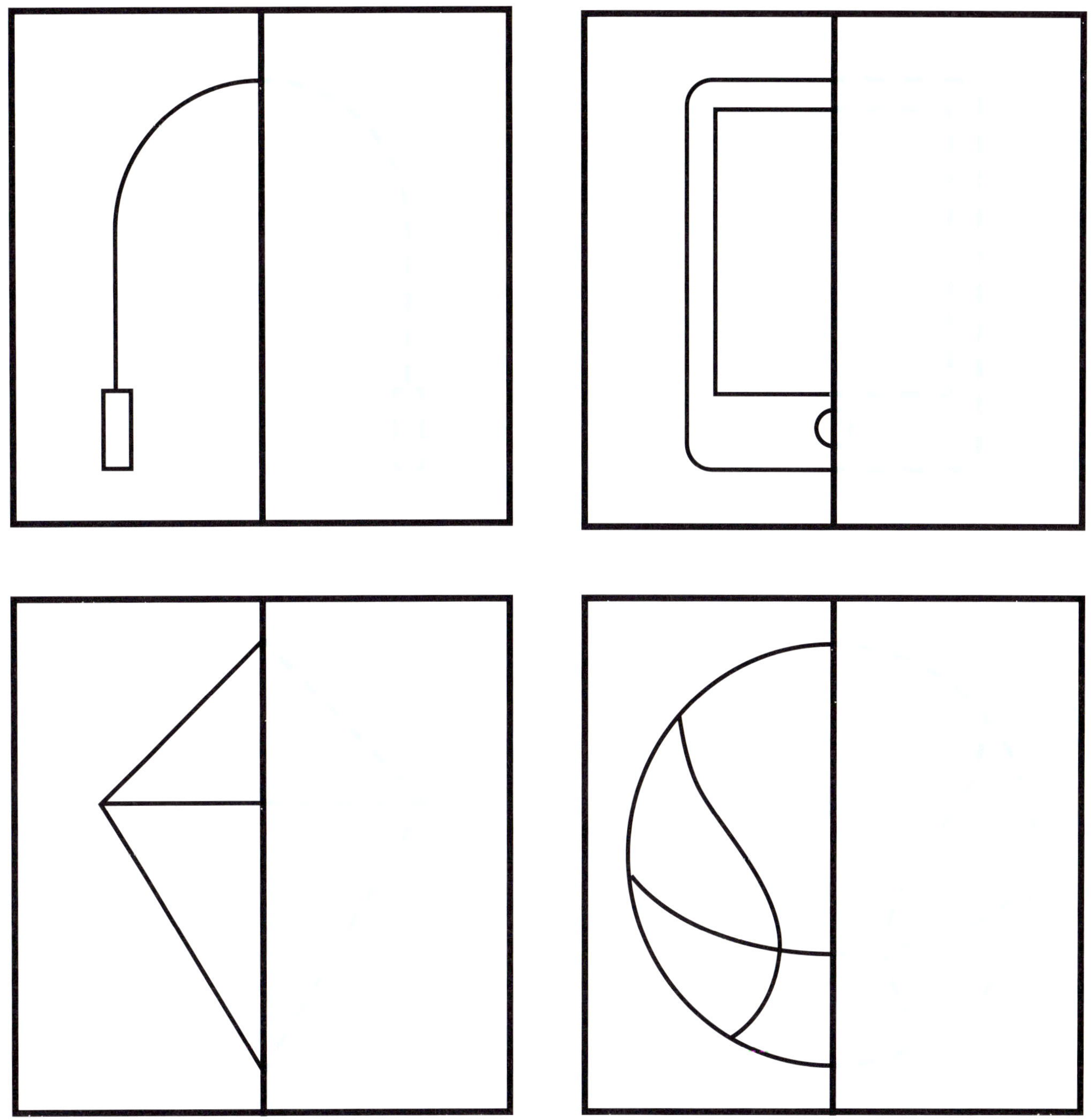

1 Trace and say. 2 Color.

Lesson 3 ○ Feelings

I'm happy

1 Who is happy? Circle and say. **2** Think and check (✓).

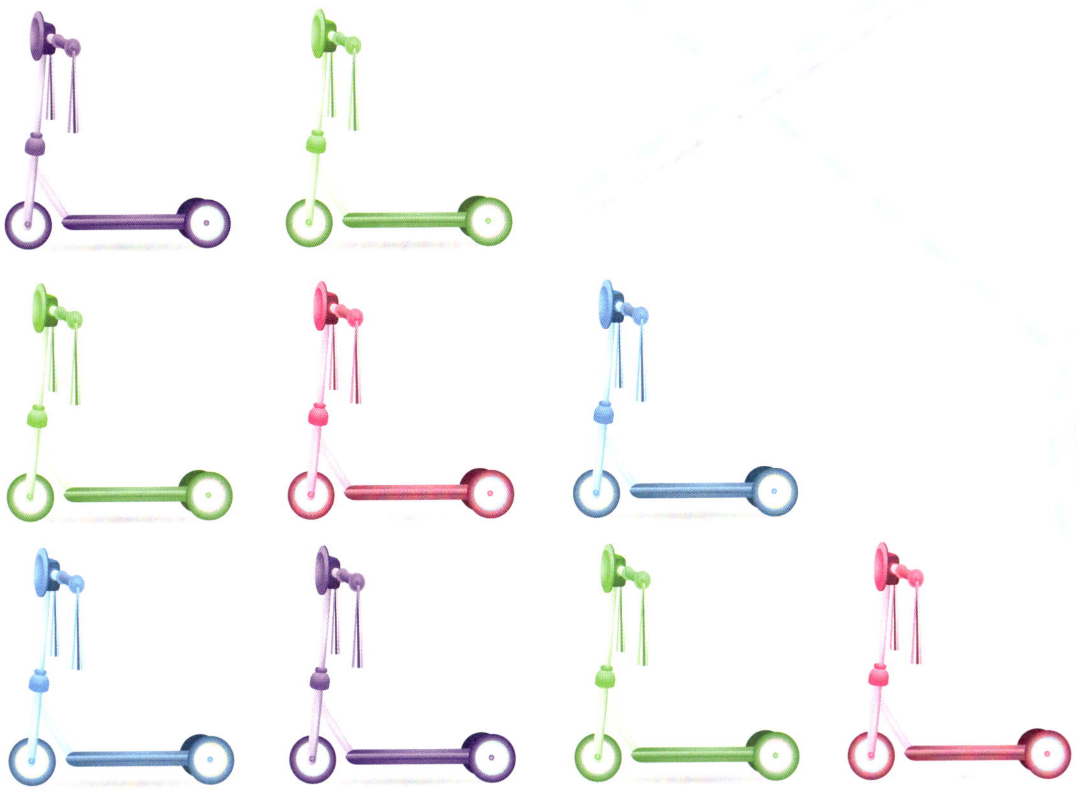

1 Count and match. 2 Trace and say.

Let's play

1 4.10 **Listen and check (✓).** 2 **Look and cross (✗).**

1 I play outside Look and circle. 2 Choose and color.

Playtime

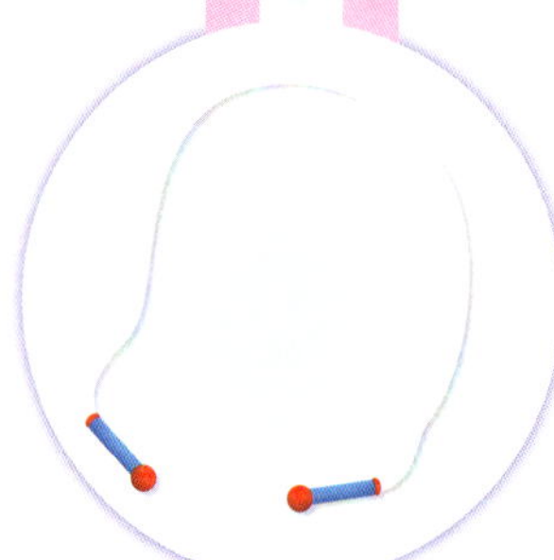

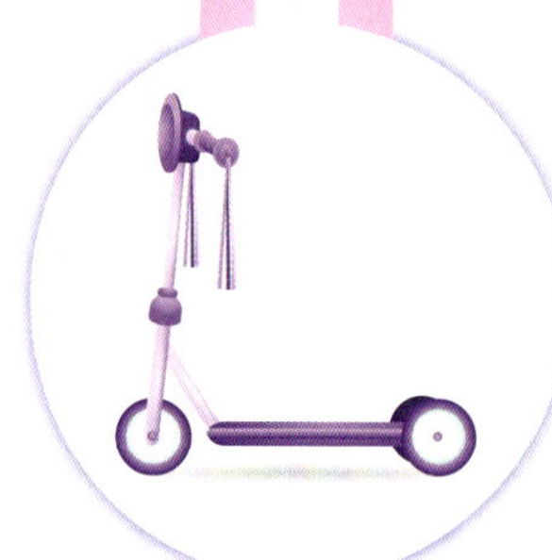

1 Draw lines. 2 Point and say.

1 🎧 4.14 Listen. Find and check (✓). 2 Color your star.

5 My lunch

① Match and say. ② Think and check (✓).

1 Trace. 2 Draw ☺ or ☹. Say.

Lesson 3 ○ Feelings

I'm thirsty

1 Who is thirsty? Circle and say. 2 Think and check (✔).

1 Color [orange] and color [purple]. 2 Say.

Russell is lost

1 5.10 Listen and check (✓). 2 Look and cross (✗).

1 I share Look and circle. 2 Choose and color.

Lunchtime

❶ **Look and match.** ❷ **Point and say.**

1 5.14 **Listen. Find and check (✓).** 2 **Color your star.**

6 My room

1 Match and say. 2 Think and check (✓).

1 Trace. 2 6.5 Listen and point. Say.

I'm upset

1 Who is upset? Circle and say. 2 Think and check (✔).

Triangle | Square

1 Trace and say.

Lesson 5A ○ Storytime

Woody helps out

1 6.11 **Listen and check (✓).** 2 **Look and cross (✗).**

1 *I help out* **Look and circle.** 2 **Choose and color.**

Bedrooms

1 Look and match. 2 Point and say.

1 6.15 **Listen. Find and check (✓).** 2 **Color your star.**

7 The farm

1 Match and say. **2** Think and check (✔).

1 Draw lines. 2 7.5 Listen and point. Say.

I'm surprised

1 Who is surprised? Circle and say. 2 Think and check (✔).

10

9

1 Count and match. 2 Trace and say.

Farm surprise!

1 🎧 7.11 **Listen and check (✓).** 2 **Look and cross (✗).**

1 *I say sorry* Look and circle. 2 Choose and color.

Farm animals

1 Look and match. 2 Point and say.

1 7.15 **Listen. Find and check (✓).** 2 **Color your star.**

8 Playground

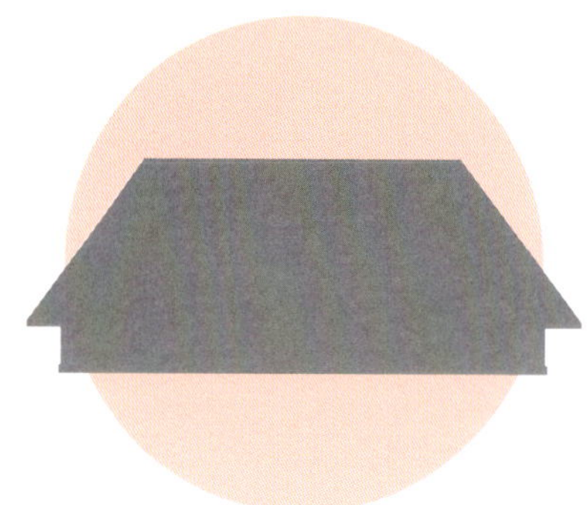

1 Match and say. 2 Think and check (✔).

I'm in the sandbox

1 Draw lines. 2 8.5 Listen and point. Say.

I'm angry

1 Who is angry? Circle and say. 2 Think and check (✓).

Brown | Pink

1 Color ● and color ●. 2 Say.

Playground fun

1 8.11 **Listen and check (✓). 2 Look and cross (✗).**

1 *I take turns* Look and circle. 2 Choose and color.

Playgrounds

1 Look and match. 2 Point and say.

1 8.15 **Listen. Find and check (✓). 2 Color your star.**

9 Actions

❶ **Match and say.** ❷ **Think and check (✓).**

1 Draw lines. 2 9.5 Listen and point. Say.

I'm tired

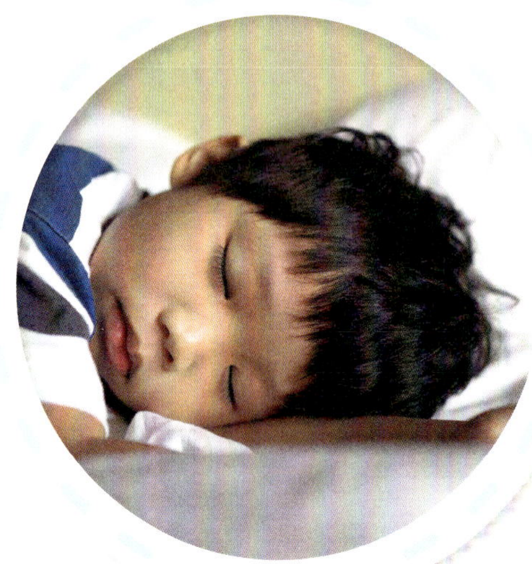

❶ Who is tired? Circle and say. ❷ Think and check (✓).

1 Color and say. 2 Trace and say.

Simba can listen

1 9.11 Listen and check (✓). 2 Look and cross (✗).

1 *I can listen* **Look and circle.** **2** **Choose and color.**

Lesson 6 ○ Real world

Active fun

1 Look and match 2 Point and say

1 9.15 **Listen. Find and check (✓). 2 Color your star.**

Unit 1

Ll

1 Look and match.

2 1.18 Listen and check. Say.

Unit 2

Rr

1 Look and match.

2 2.18 Listen and check. Say.

Unit 3 | Unit 4

Nn

Jj

1 Look and match.
2 3.18 Listen and check. Say.

1 Look and match.
2 4.18 Listen and check. Say.

Unit 5

Pp

1 Look and match.

2 5.18 Listen and check. Say.

Unit 6

Ww

1 Look and match.

2 6.19 Listen and check. Say.

Unit 7 | Unit 8

sh

1 Look and match.
2 7.19 Listen and check. Say.

ch

1 Look and match.
2 8.19 Listen and check. Say.

Unit 9

th

1 Look and match.

2 9.19 Listen and check. Say.

1 At school

2 The weather

3 My face

4 My things

5 My lunch

1 2 3 4 5 6 7 8 9 10

My learning path

Units 6–9

6 My room

7 The farm

8 Playground

9 Actions